Suffer Well
POEMS FOR THE GRIEVING
by Korie Griggs

VK PRESS
Indianapolis, IN

VK Press, LLC
PO BOX 78044
Indianapolis, IN 46278
www.vkpresses.com

Editor: Manòn Voice
Interior Design: ess mckee
Cover Design: Nathasa Rae

Library of Congress Control Number: 2022910805

First edition published October, 25, 2022
in the United States by VK Press, LLC

E-Book ISBN 979-8-218-08262-8
Paperback ISBN 978-0-9982754-9-9

Dedication

I continue to be reminded that I do not only carry my story within me. I carry the stories of those who have gone on before me. This book is for them. This book is for the ones who raised me and the ones who have loved me well. It is for the ones who made it possible for this love to persevere. To my brother, Konnor, for teaching me tenderness and compassion without ever speaking a word. To my Ma, for teaching me the belief in endless possibilities and for meeting me in my own eyes. To Mommom, for choosing me anyway. To Paw, for being the best man and father I've ever known. To Vince, for praying over my words. To Tylin, for challenging my creativity. I miss you all. May this love flowing from me meet you wherever you are.

Epigraph

It hurts to know I couldn't save you; that I couldn't love you into remission or love you out of depression

from *"What Hurts?"*

Table of Contents

FULL OF FURY

BACK AND FORTH

REDUCED TO TEARS

ROLLING WITH THE PUNCHES

TOGETHER, BUT APART

Introduction

I've said a time or two that if I were to list out my life, it would look like a series of unfortunate events. I began my intimate relationship with grief and death at eight years old. I quickly understood that the only constant in life was dying, and there was no way for my innocence to be protected from it. Survival became a daily goal in my life, and writing became the key component of my survival toolbox.

I wrote my way through my brother's death at only eight years old and six years later at my mother's deathbed. So many moments that I didn't know how I would possibly survive were survivable because of the liberating power of words. I disappeared into books and writing all through high school and college as a way to cope. Writing became an essential part of my healing journey, and it still is to this day. When I am writing, I can fully process all that is going on within me, even if I can't find all the answers I am seeking.

I do believe that I am built for surviving impossible moments. I'd never wish the depths of grief I have experienced on any person, but so many of us have felt the agony of loss. I didn't understand the full magnitude of loss and grief until I had to learn how to grieve someone that was still walking this earth. The death of my marriage wrecked me in ways that changed the course of my life forever, and for the better. Again, I wrote my way through it. I created a spoken word visual album entitled KORudos that is my survival story; up until 2021...

I suppose this book is part of my current survival story. 2021 was a year full of extraordinary loss that pushed me to live an extraordinary life. As of August 1, 2021, I fully became an orphan at the age of 31. My grandparents raised me through the rollercoaster of hospitalizations of my disabled brother and in home hospice of my mother's cancer journey. They saw me through all of my most meaningful moments: high school graduation, college, my own health scares, marriage, divorce, many moves... They chose me, showed up for me, and loved me well. It was an honor to return to Indiana to care for them.

My grandparents transitioned within one week of each other. Mommom led the way unexpectedly, and Paw followed after a few days of being cared for by myself and my two aunts. They both kept their strong spirits until the very end and exited on their own terms. It broke my heart and inspired me simultaneously.

The thickness of grief weighed heavy in the home that raised me. It was left empty all the while, their DNA dripping off every surface. They spent almost 60 years in that home, and their spirits live on through all the love they shared there. I was exhausted from caretaking. I had to get out. I went to share some drinks with two of my closest friends on the day my grandfather died. As I raised my glass to the goodness and lives of those who raised me, I received a call that no one wants to receive. One of my greatest friends, Vince "Teddy" Patton, lost his life in a drowning accident. Disbelief washed over me. I couldn't believe I was faced with more agony to survive. I had returned to Indiana to visit for a couple of days, and those couple of days ended up turning into three months. I felt the need to get out, but I knew I couldn't leave.
I needed to write.

I wrote many of these poems within the epicenter of my grief. I sat in the home that raised me, and I wrote. I screamed. I cried. I sat in complete stillness. I grieved. I suffered well. I'm proud of what flowed so beautifully from a deep place of pain. The whole process has felt essential to my healing and honoring those that have gone before me.

Grief is something so familiar and unwanted in my life. But, it has been the catalyst for so many beautiful creations. As I took the familiar journey through the stages of grief, I also found myself on a journey to peace. I can't bring back those I have lost physically, but I can feel them everywhere in spirit. I feel them through my writing and I find them there whenever I feel lost or overwhelmed. My hope is that you will find yourself less alone in your grief journey through these poems. Writing these poems was my survival guide; may words continue to lead us home.

In Rememberance

I've Never Felt a Grief So Enormous

I've never held it in the way I am now; my body is figuring out how to carry it. I really don't want to. I want to release it. I want to birth it from my depths and feel it fall out. I'm so done with it. I am so done with this grief. It doesn't have the power to consume me, but I can't seem to find the right recipe to grow around it.

I can't seem to figure out how to swallow it up rather than sit in its belly. This grief is different. It's a total loss - massive casualties.

How in the world does one walk away from all the wreckage?

Rising, rising, rising; choosing to burn alive. Taken to hell and back. A true story about making it over - making it all the way over and making it through the Storm while trudging through the Valley. Limping her way all the way to victory, because even if this lone survivor can't walk pretty she's still standing. This is the truest sight of God's peace in human form.

This is Korie's story...

Grief Creeps

When grief is no longer so fresh, it tends to take me by surprise; mostly at night, right after the sun has set. As if to remind me that I made it through another day without you. I wind down my day, take time to reflect, and that's when grief hits. I'm reminded just how much I still feel the loss of you.

I begin looking through our pictures in some faint attempt to feel close to you; sometimes, I even scroll to your name in my phone because I don't think I could ever bring myself to delete you. There's some comfort in seeing your name, and I just think about how it used to feel to call you.

Now, the grief has made itself fully known; it's no longer an undertone. I'm sitting with it; we're side by side, and as grief inches its way closer, it fully consumes my insides. I've learned to welcome it in. I even ask it to stay for a while. I don't even begin to rush its process. I've come to know that grief will always come and go, even if it sneaks up on me from time to time. I've come to know it well enough that grief no longer scares me.

Peace Prayers

Some memories never escape you, no matter how often you long for them to be replaced. One of the hardest mournings of my life was when my grandmother died. Finding her lifeless on the couch led me to speak peace into the house.

From the quiet agony of his hospice bed, my grandfather requested a prayer with all of us gathered there. Suddenly my own voice surprised me by a conversation with God that I can only slightly recall. There was a request for peace - a plea really; for a peace that could surpass all understanding.

And silently, my cries for peace to replace the memories of this mourning.

I knew one day this day would find me; you've now been gone longer than I had you. It's a strange realization. My grief over you has been part of my life longer than the mother you were to me. They say, "time heals all wounds." They say, "it gets easier with time." I don't even know who 'they' are, but I often wonder if they've ever experienced what they are proclaiming. 15 is a number that continues to multiply. Year after year while I'm still stuck chasing after memories that keep trying to escape me.

I hate the thought of even more time passing, and more memories falling through the cracks of my aging brain, but it's just the way of life to progress.

October 15 is a day I always remember. Fifteen years later, and I am still wondering what it would be like to celebrate your living rather than sitting with your dying memories. Fifteen years should feel like an incredible survival story, but I'm not celebrating.

Simply surviving without your living is no tribute in my eyes. I honor time well spent, and give thanks for the 14 years I had you; while breathing intentionally for the years to come that I now only get to remember.

I pray I never know the grief of you more than the heart of you.

The Woman Who Has Everything
My Grandmother's Eulogy

How can you give a gift to the woman who has everything? The only offering I can seem to find is a recounting of everything she birthed. Through mothering, grandmother and great-grand-mothering; year after year, managing to do it all while raising children, grandkids and great-grandbabies. A woman who worked and wived at the very same time while nurturing all despite her wellness.

 Nancy Lou showed us all the honor it is to have her as our own. A woman full of fight and hilarity. A woman full of giving and protection. A woman so strongly rooted as the basis of our family tree.

 We've grown from all she planted; some branches stretching farther than others; some fruit taking longer to ripen. Yet, here we all are despite all of the seasons and weathering. We are thankful for her; our mom, our Mommom, our Nancy Lou.

Overall Paw
My Grandfather's Eulogy

I owe my life to a man who wore overalls every day. Rather than asking why I made the assumption that it must be due to growing up in deep Mississippi or always prioritizing comfortability.

My only answer can now be found in the deeper realizations about why I find myself wearing them so often. Overalls are really great when you've got to carry a lot, and my Paw carried it all. He carried his entire family, even after his death.

I like to imagine each pocket filled up. Each person he loved would find something different due to the love he showed so uniquely. There has got to be close to a million lessons lining each pocket and seam. There are hard days of labor, late-night snacks, paintbrushes, sawdust, oil stains, and pages from books to fix anything and everything.

If you turned his pockets inside out, the well of love would fill up the entire Mississippi Bottom just past Griggs Rd. In each water droplet, you'd see the family he cherished blended with boyhood stories that became parables with crinkled recipes for tomato soup and fried bologna sandwiches. Now we all overflow from lessons full of humor and love poured out over our lifetimes.

I'll keep filling my pockets with the wisdom of Paw's legacy that I carry.

Phone Calls From Heaven

I answered my phone in my sleep one night. It was one of those dreams that was tethered to reality. It was "Vince Teddy" on the screen. My excitement didn't allow me to question how that could be.

As my tears began to stream, I told him how sad I was from missing those I love. He offered me laughter with words I'll never forget:

Just keep living and you'll find us there always; in your breath and your laugh, but mostly in your creation.

My lungs filled with the largest breath of wonder for where he must be. *I'm in the groove, KP. You already know.* But all I could do was imagine while his joy carried me through to strength before the line was disconnected.

Epitaphs

Grief elicits some unexpected thoughts. I find myself thinking about epitaphs more than most while wishing we gave more flowers to the living rather than returning to graveyards for memories. If I passed my marker today, I'd want my epitaph to say:

SHE WAS SUNSHINE AND RAIN SIMULTANEOUSLY.

4855928

Every number I've ever known to call home is now disconnected. If I called familiar numbers, I'd meet a stranger's voice or a dial tone.

I think I finally know how orphans must feel; they really have nowhere to go and can only take what they can carry with them. Lucky for me, I can carry a lot. So, here I am packing up one more time; getting ready for a journey unknown.

At least I'll never forget the number that leads to home.

A Letter to Those Who Love Me

On a warm day, while walking through a cemetery, I reflected on what really matters to me. I had my first new friend in my old hometown by my side. Walking amongst the no longer living will give you feelings of reminiscing. Neither of us could have possibly known that he would be joining The Other Side in four years. We stumbled upon a "Before I Die" wall with markings of others who also thought about who they wanted to be and the life they wanted to lead.

Should I die before you believe it's my time, I have a few rules and regulations before you decide to lose your mind. (I've been there; I know it can happen).

First, take a breath. Then, give thanks for that breath; because we both know you never know if your next one is promised. Second, take some time to close your eyes. Think back to a memory we made. Laugh and cry at the same time; in only the way I ever knew how. Third, and only when you're ready, take a piece of me to a place where you believe I'd like to eternally rest. Fourth, live. Live so boldly and loudly that you have no regrets whenever it's time for us to meet again.

Lastly, but far from the least, love. Love hard and well. Love with a fierceness that leaves no questions to the ones you have to leave behind. Enjoy all the days, try new things, fall down and get back up, cry it out, laugh out loud, believe in hope and be proud that you've made it this far. I'm nothing but proud of the person you are.

Seasons

I live every season of life as if it will be my last;

No wonder I miss them so much.

Shooting Stars

Sometimes I fall asleep watching the stars while wondering if you find me there. I see you in each constellation; complicated and scattered. The moon seems to hang in a way that I've never noticed before, and I'm reminded that things are not always as they may seem.

I no longer feel a pain in my heart in the place you used to fill. We no longer know each other; a reality I never fully believed would be true. Yet, somehow we're still connected in a universe all its own. I opened my eyes to admire more stars, and saw one shooting just for you; didn't break me. Every moment you thought I was destroyed I came back even stronger. Remember when you told me that I could never live happily?

I just want you to know that you were wrong. Sometimes I wonder if the stars remind you of the night you almost killed me. As if vanishing stars represent the joy you tried to take from me. Rather than burning out I sparked to life, and you missed out on a beautiful one.

I'm not sorry; we all make choices in this life. I'm happy for me. I'm happy that this first wasn't my last. I'm happy that I get to know healthy love. I'm happy that I get to think about the possibility of a future that is just as bright as me.

Past Tense

I'm having the hardest time talking about you in the past tense, because I feel you everywhere. Even though I can't see you again, every move I make now feels like a dedication. I'm charged with carrying on our dreams. I accept this obligation. We will meet at the top, but you're already there, preparing a place for whenever we get to meet again.

It's just that; no one ever told me that missing you would last a lifetime.

An Ode to An Indiana Fall Night

The scent of stale bonfire on my clothes and hair always gives me a feeling of home. Leaves on the ground, walnuts crashing down, fire embers making their way up smoke tunnels to the stars. No picture can begin to capture a moment such as this. Love embodied, a glimpse of heaven, that feeling of complete knowing; that even if only for some moments, everything is truly alright on this beautiful fall night.

My Grandpa's Hands

My grandpa's hands could create so many somethings from endless nothings. His hands reached out and comforted when you least expected and always needed. Those same hands that took the wheel to teach and guide also intertwined for prayer at the bedside. My grandpa's hands are the biggest and strongest I've ever known.

My memory floods with moments where I tried on his rings. Amazement filled my whole body as I took in the encompassing size when placed upon my own hands. My grandpa's hands never felt calloused due to the gentle spirit that accompanied them. It was so strange never feeling anything rough while knowing all the work they are doing. My grandpa's hands have carried more weight than I can even begin to imagine. They hold memories that can be passed on for generations.

My grandpa's hands are the hands of a hero, and my hero knew my name. I'll always remember my grandpa's hands because I now see that mine are the same.

Aftershock

I've filled a syringe with .25 mg so many times it's committed to my muscle memory. Every hour morphine: every four hours Valium-just to make you comfortable. It's an unsettling feeling when your home becomes a hospital room. Your doors stay unlocked most days because someone is always coming and going. It's an endless game of hurry up and wait.

I feel like I should still be staying up all night to care for you. I still wake up at times and think I should be checking your breathing patterns. I find myself staring at your chair; it feels like you're still here. As if we can continue in conversation because you've never really left. I can't bring myself to leave the space where you once were. I know I won't find you there.

I witnessed your last breath. No one tells you how to walk someone to death and then keep on living, or that you'll drive yourself crazy watching the rise and fall of a chest full of labored breaths.

A Letter to My Unborn Child

We haven't met yet, and maybe we never will, but my heart longs for you while my body stays in worry about your possibility. I often think about what it would be like to raise you, but if the opportunity never comes, that will be okay too. I just want you to know that I have enough love inside of me for you. I have room for you. I will allow you to grow while always making sure that you know how loved you are in a moment, even before I ever knew you.

My longing for you comes from longing for my mother. I will teach you who she was, and we can both grow to know her through one another.

With this love, you'll always be protected.

This Can't Be Real!

The Lies We Tell

It's as if we want all to be well, so we tell ourselves lie after lie in hopes we can become our own clever disguise. You're allowed to be unhappy with where you are, but if you never admit it to yourself or anyone around, how can you ever change your current state?

Stop telling others what you think they want to hear when your actions are always speaking louder than the words touching ears. Scream it out loud if you must; I'M UNHAPPY HERE! I'd rather hear you scream it than feel the subtle ache in the day to day.

The sound of your joy with me and for me is becoming only a fond memory. Change can occur at an alarming rate, or a slow progression, the erosion of lie after lie finally breaks down– the truth of it all. I never knew I forced something on you until it was too late, but when every question you ask is met with a lie, how are you supposed to adequately articulate it?

It seems like it should be simple; cause and effect, but it's too hard to read when the truth isn't intact. I just hope one day we stop believing all the lies we tell. They really serve no one, not even ourselves.

Mourning in the Evening

I swear I've spent the better part of two years readying myself for a grief I didn't think my heart could possibly contain. Preparation hasn't helped me much.

I returned home for the one grief that hasn't even happened yet; Instead, I was met with a mountain of grief that has me standing so still in my tracks that I wonder if I'll ever be able to move again.

My own inner dialogue begins to feel like an extended interrogation for a crime that can never be solved.

We went from finding our rhythm to everything feeling out of tune. My grandmother raised us to show up to life on our own terms and proved it with the sneak attack of her own death.

I didn't think I needed any more tough love lessons. I've learned so much from her living, and now feel the complete ripple effect of her dying, fierce until the very end. I'm continuously learning the good stock that I come from; I just can't seem to process it all yet.

Every time the night falls, I'm reminded that you never know what the mourning will bring.

Grieving Three

My heart can't even begin to feel all that each pain holds, and my mind can't begin to fully unravel this grief braid that's been woven. Each strand somehow continues to get tighter with each passing day, while simultaneously unraveling in places I didn't even know existed.

I'm sleeping less than ever before and drinking more. I'm finding ways to cope with this new reality that I still refuse to fully believe because there's just no way I'm supposed to navigate this much grief, and simply be okay.

It feels like when reaching out to touch my family tree that an entire branch has fallen off, and I'm looking and examining only to realize that the tree seems to be hollowing from the inside out. This is hollow grief because it's leaving me feeling abandoned from the inside out.

I can't even begin to imagine a world without these three members of my family. I feel like I've adopted a complete orphan mentality. I no longer know where I will run when the whole world seems to be crashing down.

All of these homes are becoming houses, and only energy remains to fill the empty spaces where all our memories were made. This is truly my greatest battle yet, survival of the fittest. It may just be easier to cut it all off at the roots rather than try to unravel all of these truths.

The Stillness of This Night

There's a lack of stillness now every night; no comfortability in sight. Maybe it's just grief from eyes draining all night with no relief. The headaches from crying and flushed cheeks; good grief seems to be the difference these days. No longer delaying feeling all of it; each wave, unsteady breath, sinking feeling, float back to the top. Every step of the way, here I am living to tell about it, while those I love fade away.

Aging

Aging as a woman is strange; so many moments of unfamiliarity, moments of dissatisfaction with the body I live within. Searching for beauty in a face that looks back at me while simultaneously struggling to accept the body that houses me. I used to feel pretty, beautiful, huggable, lovable, physical.

I don't always recognize who I see looking back at me. As if I have become only a memory. Refusal of accepting the inevitable, eventually, but not just yet.

Full of Fury

Panic

It's brewing ever so slowly, then without warning it all begins to boil over. The overwhelming feelings about nothing and everything intrude. Sitting within the cold while longing for warmth. Shedding tears while hoping the heat of my anger will dry them rapidly. Feeling endlessly lonely while knowing that I'm never alone.

A strong mind with a fragile heart creates a self-contained hurricane as waves of grief swell in my insides. There's a longing to be held by all the arms that are long gone. My heart breaks the more it beats. Questions begin to scream but never seem to make it outside my mind.

Who wants to hear these thoughts?
Who wants to read these words?
Who wants to be strong while feeling weak?
Who nurtures the healers?

And now I can't breathe. Searching for freedom and protection as my heart begins to race. My body begins to react to the emotional flight, and my legs start to ache. Reaching out for embrace with no knowledge of my needs. All these words can't formulate the wants.

B   R   E   A   T   H   E

That's what I've forgotten to do. This pillow absorbs my tears as sleep longs to greet me. This panic will not consume me. I am here.

Preparing for Deployment

I feel like I'm being prepared for deployment, like I gotta get away from everything I love to stay safe. Because if I stay in this current wreckage there won't be anything left to salvage. This home turned into a house right before my eyes, and its bones carry the memories of every person I've ever loved. How can the only home I've ever known suddenly become a place of ruins barely recognizable? I keep thinking that if everything just stayed the same, I could always walk back into this time capsule, and feel some kind of safety, but the ones with the open arms are gone now. Only ghosts walk these halls while their spirits live on through these parables. I never knew a heart could continue beating after so much breakage, but here I stand, breathing it all in for what could possibly be the end. Because once you leave home for the last time there really is nowhere left to return.

That Night

I'll never forget the night it all made sense. I'll never forget the night I said, "alright." I'll never forget the night. I'll never forget the night you held a gun to your head and said, *"I'm just going to shoot myself in front of you so you have to live with the sight of that for the rest of your life."*

I'll never forget that night.

I stared at you for what felt like enough time for each star to be stripped from the sky that created this darkest night. You stared back with your threatening look with the words still dripping from your lips. You knew each one would cut and hurt, but you knew you didn't care. Maybe you really would rather be dead. The last time I looked in your eyes was after you said those words.

I can never forget that night.

I'll never forget the night I walked away. I walked away from you, in that moment, in that trance, from those words; and I walked out the door. I shut it and only heard silence. What you don't know about that night is that I stood outside the door long enough to know if you would pull the trigger and if I would hear the sound that would echo through my ears for the rest of my days.

I'll never forget that night.

I'll never forget that night because that's the night I said goodbye to the love of my life and a piece of my heart. I can't get that night back. I can't get those pieces back. I can't get that piece of myself back.

I can't get that innocence back. I can't get the sight out of my mind, because I can never forget that night. And you don't even believe that it happened. But, congratulations, you've impacted me for the rest of my life. I'll never forget that night because even though you didn't pull the trigger, that's the night you died and the night I was given new life.

Blinded Layers

Stop with the *"I'm just tryin' to get to know ya"* trope when we both know that's not what you want. I promise you're not ready to peel me back layer by layer. You can't possibly understand all the tears I have cried over men just like you, who claim they want to get to know me, and after the first layer are too scared to pull back to layer two. Tears over men who get to layer two and realize grief isn't something they can sign up for, so why bother with peeling away to layer three. Tears over men who see that layer three is a battle ground that I've conquered, so I must be strong enough to endure another war, and I don't need anyone around for more healing, so it's okay to walk out the door. They never bother to think about layer four. Tears over a man who made it to layer four, five, six and seven all while entertaining other women. But who am I to take away your choice? My tears blinded me. I fell so in love with the potential of him that I couldn't see the dark reality.

DeadSea

                                    afloat,
I really believed I could keep you   but you didn't care if
that meant I would
                  sink.

You taught me that some men only grow enough to notice
their own ignorance, but not enough to change it.

RUMBLE

Maybe you're created to do something about everything you're
angry about. There's a rumble in my Spirit, a roar that wants to
escape deep from the depths of me. A mourning feeling like
the pounding of a thousand drums. The collective sound of the
mothers reaching out as their sons leave the house. Do you
worry when you jog down the street? Do you feel your heart
skip beats as your partner leaves? Do you think twice about
how you speak? DO you feel these pains of grief?

I feel a rumble in my Spirit, and I'm terrified to hear
it escape. It will leave my lips as a scream, bellowing from
the depths of me. WHO GIVES YOU THE RIGHT TO TAKE
ANOTHER PERSON'S LIFE? But my voice won't even be loud
enough to cut through all the noise. I've got this rumble in my
Spirit; an ache I can never escape. We should not have to live
our lives afraid to simply jog down the street.

AUMAUD ARBERY
AUMAUD ARBERY
AUMAUD ARBERY

I rumble for you.

BREONNA

You deserved more than some loop-holed sad excuse for
justice.

You should be here.

You are the breath and heart still beating in every Black
Woman in this world.

We are you.
You are us.

You should be here.

>No justice; no peace.
>Breonna was killed in her sleep.
>
>No justice; no peace.
>Brett Hankison,
>Jonathan Mattingly,
>Myles Cosgrove,
>YOU SHOULD NOT BE FREE.
>
>NO JUSTICE;
>
>NO PEACE.

Equal Parts
A Poem Inspired by Stylistic Nikki Giovanni

If there was a bag to hold all of my emotions it would be
overflowing and spilling out of holes from all the ones with the
sharp edges I wouldn't recommend putting your hand inside
or even attempting to understand because right next to sadness
you'll find joy and right next to anger you'll find euphoria
and right next to unrest you'll find resilience and right next to
tired you'll find bravery that I didn't even know could exist if
I could only begin to understand what it's like to experience
every emotion at once and not even one more than the other
but a completely simultaneous experience that I didn't even
know one person was capable to hiding this bag so full of
magic

Somehow, I gotta learn to unpack and hopefully begin
to stand up a little straighter because I refuse to allow all of the
happy feelings produced from hard work to be diminished by
the world that doesn't want to see Black Women win let alone
live

Yesterday found me with the most unsurprising and
heartbreaking news sandwiched between all of the goodness I
could ever hope to receive all because I refuse to be a statistic
I refuse to be a number I refuse to be anything less than the
purpose that rumble and beats inside of my chest

There are tears staining my face now getting trapped in
the wrinkles that my smile creates but for now you just get the
stoic face of a woman who continues to create

I'll allow myself the privilege of rest because
somewhere along the way that's what my ancestors also
prayed for thinkin' these feelings ain't everything these feelings
are just the tip of more of something so much more of a new
beginning.

Sentence Breathing

Yesterday the cops were stopping every car and checking licenses. It scared me. I felt my chest tighten. I couldn't get myself to breathe regularly. I felt angry. I felt sad. I felt frustrated. I felt hot tears begin to form in the corners of my eyes. I thought, *there's no way I'm gonna let them see me cry.* I breathed deeply. I listened carefully. A routine traffic stop can quickly turn into hashtags and caskets. I didn't ask any questions. I have a million questions. I can't stop thinking about Breonna Taylor in her bed. I should be asleep. I never stop thinking about Breonna Taylor in her bed. I should really be sleeping. I can't stop thinking about Breonna Taylor in her bed. I just can't sleep. Some nights I stay awake listening and praying for her family. There will never be justice. I don't want to stop my car. I don't want to show my license. My life will not be policed. My joy will not be policed. I think I'm finally breathing regularly. I must go to sleep.

How Long is a Sentence

Get ready because this will be a run on that means never ending if you know where I'm coming from because it should be never ending but even never ending doesn't equal justice for a life that was taken in an act too reckless I can't say senseless because I know that man's mind was intact when he continued to kneel on George Floyd's neck and let me guess you think we should be "over it" by now because a sentencing has been released but I don't think I'll ever "get over it" because there are too many "its" that we are supposed to "get over" and 22.5 years just isn't long enough when there are brothers sisters mamas papas just so many sitting within this country's prison system for something as simple as possession 30 plus years some of them but murder only gets you just past the legal drinking age 22.5 years isn't even half of George Floyd's life it's close but that don't matter because what actually matters is that a sentence should never end when you take another's life the grieving doesn't get to end the trauma doesn't end the memories don't get to end the feelings and emotions wrapped up in every heartbeat that took to the streets to scream and cry and say each and every name but just let me take a breath because the inhale and the exhale are the only way I can talk to God these days and that's the only way I can sit and not scream because there's no timeline that justifies taking our lives.

Aries

I've apologized for my existence more times than the years I've been alive. Sometimes I feel like I'm burning alive; as if something has been lit within the depths of me, and it's slowly making its way through all of my extremities. I wish to harness this feeling, but it's so fleeting. It comes and goes with the moon phases. I wait for its return and prepare myself by holding only embers of the fires that lost their momentum within me.

Irritation

At times I find myself irritated by the complicated lies that my human brain likes to feed me from time to time. The only person that expects perfection is the one looking back at me in this reflection. Only I hold the ultimate expectation for everything to be done solely by me, and in a timely fashion. I'd tell anyone else to extend some grace or show some compassion, but here I am just being my worst weapon. Why am I being so mean to this being when it continues to show up and house me? I must show up for me the same way I show up for others. This shouldn't feel like advanced level chemistry, but there must be something shaking up in my biology.

Staring at the Color Wheel
Inspired by Coffee

I've heard more compliments over the tasting of a coffee than I ever have for a Black man. We indulge and receive while even taking the time to describe our experience in hopes of others having a similar one.

He is yellow with every reason to have hints of pink, magenta, peach or coral.

I receive sweet, mellow, and delicate all too familiar, yet unseen while hearing descriptions of bitter, harsh and caustic. How are we having such a different experience? Every time I take a sip, I think of him.

There's an easy correlation. A way to take time and reflect on all Black bodies see, hear and feel past what meets the eye.

If you can take the time for your morning cup surely you can take time for the marginalized.

Back and Forth

Cemetery Wonder

I can't be where I want to be because it's too cold, but I'm here anyway. I leave pennies for the thoughts and nickels for the nods. There's a new flower at her gravesite, and I wonder who misses her as much as I do. I wonder why I come here and cry alone. I wonder why I hold my own hand to find comfort. I wonder if there's a way to let her know how much I love her. I wonder if I'll ever be able to allow someone to see all my darkness. I wonder if anyone will want to be my light when I am dim. I wonder if I'll always have to be the strong one. I wonder if I'll be the one who fills the space in the ground between my mother and brother because there's only room for one.

Today is heavy and full of pain. My eyes are faucets, and I don't know where to go because I don't find home in places. I find home in people. So, what can this grave really bring me? The love isn't tangible here, and I don't know where else to spiral out of control. I'll just sit a little longer, hoping the cold will numb me long enough for wonder to escape me for a while.

Grief Pools

Sometimes it feels like I'm just wading in the waters. It's always peaceful in those moments, like basking in the sunshine while ankle deep in the shallow end. Feeling all of the beauty in the midst of all the pain in a perfect and simultaneous existence. Then, it's as if a storm rolls in, and I'm suddenly thrown into the deep with no resources to reach the surface other than my own inner fight. Sometimes I just allow the water to surround me in hopes to conserve some energy. I know the sun will shine again once the clouds clear.

Ghost Kingdom

I've created worlds inside of my mind. I remember writing stories and feeling that they were secrets I had to hide. *My dad was a rich man who traveled often but loved me well. He was gonna give me the fanciest of cars to drive.* Of course, that was all a lie, but no one actually knew there were endless possibilities when I had time to think about the other half of me.

I loved my family; still do, but there was always something missing. My imagination became so comforting. I was fully seen and understood by all my kingdom's characters. They knew me, and I knew them without a single question. This world I created came from the depths of my wonder. *Where are the people that look like me? Do they look for me too? Are they somewhere within this kingdom of myself?* A child's mind is a beautiful place to be, but what happens when those memories can't be escaped while living an adult reality?

I still think of the people I was able to create. They are my ghosts, living within a kingdom all my own.

Talking to the Moon

Sometimes when I'm watching the stars, I want to begin naming them after memories as some kind of remembrance ceremony; for everything that couldn't be. Maybe if they hold the names of everything I miss I can at least count on comfort through the night; under this blanket of everything I can no longer touch. Then, the moon reminds me ever so sweetly, *"don't get too good at being alone."* A black mirror reflecting my present struggle between a life well lived and time well spent. Is a lonely life capable of also being a full life? Is an impactful life a lonely feeling? It might be possible to spend too much time with your thoughts that you become them, rather than actually living them. No one wants to die alone, but we all do…I don't think the moon requires any response, but here I am trying to find answers for it.

Tangled Roots

I can't leave until you let me because my body can't bend in a
way that allows me to get out of whatever position I've agreed
to be in.
At some point, we find ourselves deeply rooted;
in someone, something, some place, and over time the roots
begin to show.
Maybe we don't want or need to be as deeply rooted as we
once were.

The Shortest Love Story

He loved who he loved;
I loved who I loved.
The trickiest part of falling in love is loving who we loved
apart.

Perseverance

It's everywhere. In the air thick with despair, it fills up our lungs without warning. It's in the soil that absorbs every heavy footstep we continue to take. It's in the way the sky lets loose as if it can no longer contain the pain of the world, but that's what we call rain. I see it in my own eyes from time to time, and I feel it in the chest when my heart pulses somewhat irregularly, but that's what we call a beat.

I sometimes think about how it will all feel again when the phone rings with news of another one gone too soon, but that's what we call fear. I never want to let go, but that's what we call grieving-this holding on tight even after loss, but that's what we call love persevering.

Quarantine

I've noticed that I wake up differently than ever before. I immediately check my breathing just to ensure that nothing has changed. If a cough creeps in, just lay me under a blanket of anxiety. I feel my body to see how it's responding hoping that it's feeling refreshed rather than twinged with illness. I keep a running list of groceries that I seem to always need. I know for certain I am out of coffee to drink, but I have too much anxiety to enter a store.

What if this movement is what changes everything?

What if I feel my breathing change while sickness creeps into my body?

I'm experiencing so much fear. I'm already learning to trust through fears of the unknown. I'd rather not add to that experience by fighting for life in a hospital bed all alone. I can't understand humanity not understanding the severity. There are so many bodies whose survival rate is minimal because of how they were designed. Imagine living already being a fight before a pandemic even arrived. Think past yourself for just a few moments. There's time to decide before stepping outside. We've never lived in a world like this. I understand that it doesn't make sense, but we're beginning to see that the only way to lend a helping hand is by staying away.

Vaccinated

What a taboo topic and I understand why. Historically speaking, vaccines haven't had our best interest in mind. I never thought I'd have to evaluate what I fear more: possibly dying from Covid 19 or potentially risking my life in hopes of not contracting something capable of taking away more than a year of life without even being contracted.

I can't help but think back on all the time that has passed. I lay on a couch struggling to breathe, not from a disease but from crippling anxiety, all from going outside. But progress has occurred because today, my breath is even, full of confidence and gratitude. My fears have lessened, and I've been enjoying the outside from time to time. We still live in a masked society, and none of us could have guessed this reality, but here we are. For better or worse, whatever you may choose. I choose the lesser evil in my mind.

2020 was the year the world changed. There's a long list of names from this pandemic to police brutality. There always seems to be a choice to make. All I know is I want to know where I stood whenever they retell the history.

Mirror Mirror

Imagine driving home in silence due to the last five hours of your life feeling like an out-of-body experience. Your worlds collided, but it wasn't catastrophic. It felt familiar and lonely all at once. It felt like being somewhere you've never been while being home at the same exact time. You met yourself where you used to be rather than who you have grown to become. You made yourself laugh despite the tears, and you dried up some of that well.

Trauma teaches you to be proud of how far you have come. When your whole body aches from wanting to escape you somehow still make it to the next day with adequate time for recovery. In the marathon of life, you must ready yourself for the moments where you'll run out of breath. Stop and rest. In the moments of rest is where you can see more of the world. You can see more of yourself. You can hear the pains and joys that surround you. You can learn what works; what fits and what doesn't. In these moments of rest, you grow.

As you learn to hope for a better and brighter tomorrow and make the walk back to your body you can mend the trauma trigger that found you. It all begins with breath, and then a step. You're moving again. You're moving in the direction you're intended with the memory of the version of yourself that would have given up when the pain cut too deep. You're not there anymore. That person is a stranger, and there's no need to pay any visits.

You've learned strength, bravery, and resilience while that former self stayed stagnant, afraid and persecuted for being everything that you are now proud to be. Don't allow yourself to become distracted. Stay focused. You're now well loved and there's no room for selfish reciprocity. You haven't seen this stranger in years, but you may see them from time to time in your mirror. Say goodbye. Allow that presence to be your reminder of the you that has always been inside. No one has the power to take your becoming away from you.

Re-entry

The feelings rattling around my insides are dancing the jive while singing the blues. All of the weighted feelings from saying 'see you later' to the faces of joyous missed faces create a self-isolated shell in hopes of protecting myself and those that love me. After so many harsh seasons, it's time to welcome the gentle ones. The only way to ease the transition is to enter into it again and again.

~~Don't~~ Can't Worry

You can't worry about what you don't know. There is so much left unseen, and you can't know what hasn't yet been revealed. You're just left wondering.

Why?

What's next?

But you have no business thinking about anything more than the here and now. The human brain is a funny thing. We often end up standing in our own way. As if worry and fear have ever served us well, but we will find ourselves bending to those emotional wills here and there. That's the thing about humanity; it's more fleeting than spirituality. We can go as far as Spirit leads when we don't allow our brains to trick us.

It's more about the can't rather than the don't. But what do I really know? I'm just a poet who's still learning how to know it.

Reduced to Tears

Operation

Sometimes I   wonder if I'd
feel healed if I had a heart
transplant. As if replacing the current
heart would
somehow make me feel less broken.
I just need a house call
for emotional
procedures
such as
this.

What Hurts?

It hurts to know that I couldn't save you, I couldn't love you into remission or love you out of depression. It hurts that I only got glimpses of who you were and now have to put together broken pieces to do a nonsensical puzzle. It hurts still feeling like your breath was somehow connected to mine, while still being here experiencing this plane of existence.

It hurts that I can't quite name the pain because I'm still just trying to get to know it. It hurts, but I'm living to heal through it.

A Not So Funny Story

Today I realized what felt like a million little things. A million little pieces finally fell together to give me a memory that allows my brain to feel more in sync.

My mother was depressed; why wouldn't she be? Her only daughter looked just like her, only several shades darker. Her only son never had a moment of peace until he died. Her body gave up on her; cancer took over her life. And these are just facts known to be true. There's plenty still left in

FILE UNKNOWN: Full of things I'll never get to know.

When I read the facts about her life, I start to list facts about my own.

I'm depressed; why wouldn't I be? I was born to a family who didn't look like me; to a father who has never wanted to claim me. I didn't get to live with my mother because of my little brother, but what could be changed? Nothing's normal when a six-year-old dies, and all of life's complexities sit far outside normalcy.

I was eight when my brother died, and once twelve hits, I had a mother riddled with cancer. A mother who lied about having cancer; all because she couldn't even face it. There's nothing normal about a teenager forced to bury her mother after a two-year battle with cancer; and to think that was all before even learning to drive.

I'm depressed; sometimes, but that's not the definition of who I am.

When It Catches Up with You

You can't stop the release; you let the tears roll while your
breath catches. We've been grieving our whole lives.
When we need to quench our thirst, the water comes
from our eyes. Ancestral hopes manifesting in the hearts of the
living. Yet somehow, we can't seem to catch our breath.
This story has been written even when we're too afraid
to turn the page. There's no way of knowing what lies ahead.
Grief is the only constant.
Some were built to be the strength of the tribe while
breaking little by little when the levy finally breaks, but it's
okay. Release.

When it catches up with you your heart can't help but break.

Dive

It feels like I'm trying to make my way to the surface from the deepest depths. I can see everyone above me floating and enjoying the sunshine while I'm struggling to join them. I've been underwater longer than my lungs can bear, but no one seems concerned. The surface must be near. I can see the sunshine glistening through the water, and the temperature of the water begins to change. I'm swimming, but I'm so tired. I'm ready to float.

I might need someone to dive down because this might be the first time, I can't save myself.

Where'd You Go?

The search has been relentless,
with no sign of life for days;
until a moment where I catch a glimpse of the me,
I used to be.
I was beginning to believe she may have gone away forever.

Fight Off Your Demons

Why must it always be one or the other? Black or white? Up or down? Happy or sad? Right or wrong? Stay or go? Good or bad? Open or closed?

WHY?

Because choices matter. Choices determine everything. There is always a choice. We choose every day to do something, to say something, to be something.

What about the times when you feel like you don't have a choice? The moments when you're scared, stuck, trapped, immobile, frozen.

Depression doesn't always give the option of choice. Depression can force itself upon you and take over your body. It shines its fluorescent light on all insecurities. You cry and then try repetitively, but it doesn't stop the agony. It's there in the dark when there's no sleep. It creeps into your chest to hold in laughs. It's not your friend, although it is a close companion. It's the demon that lurks in the dark corners of your mind, and it's time to fight.

Depression

If given a choice, I'd choose
fear over depression any day.
I'd rather be scared than fear
for my life.

Case of the Mondays

It was just another Monday,
but I woke up to the sound of heartbreak
and a home falling apart.

                    Now, every week is singing the Blues.

Rolling With the Punches

A First Conscious Moment of Strength

Right before her ninth birthday, her mother buried her youngest child. He was her only son. Her mother held her living child in her arms as tight as she could, and that child held back every tear. She patted her back and let her cry. She stood strong out of necessity, with no understanding as to why.

In that moment, a solid eight-year-old pillar of strength was built to hold together the mess that I proudly call my mother.

A Memory

My mom lied a lot, so I learned to love liars at a very young age. There's just something about loving someone who's learning to love themselves.

The Thing About Death

We seem to view death as an end, but what if it is a new beginning when you die. Like stepping into new ways while viewing new places; being somewhere you've never been before. As if we just visit a city amidst the clouds, a place that looks so familiar although we have never been.

For now, we only get glimpses. The view with our feet on the ground is different from the sky we see while looking down.

This Home is Now a House

There are no extra noises or quiet footsteps. The nights
are tranquil, with no snoring sounds. All of the seats find
themselves empty, yet a fullness still hangs in the air. The
familial DNA is all over these walls. The Spirit of Love still
remains. The home wasn't made from all these things inside.
The home was made from the laughter and holiday cheer. It
was made from the tough conversations that sometimes end in
tears. It was made from the dreams being supported no matter
where they may lead. It was made from all of the hard work
to ensure bright futures for all. Home was made from all the
open arms ready to greet you when you arrive.

Everything that made this house a home no longer
remains, but the foundation somehow still remains strong.

Untitled Love

My first love was a seven-year season filled with seasons that didn't always change as I did. Seasons that I learned and adjusted to. In my first love I didn't know who I was without it, but I've now learned who I am. I've learned how to operate without dependency. I've grown and created a strong and resilient soul.

Even in the resiliency I am an extremely emotional being that loves hard while wearing her heart on her sleeve. A being so extroverted about the emotions, feelings and needs of others while being introverted about her own. The last time I truly gave my heart it was taken advantage of and picked apart.

I can admit that I have intimacy issues, and sometimes I am scared to say what I am thinking due to the fear of response. Regardless of how hard I try there are still past demons I must continue to fight. Self Saratoga is my familiar friend. We work well together to a voice vulnerability, but I no longer desire self-destruction. I don't want to run. I want to legitimately know and be known. I fight to be open while combating the fear of my magic being touched by dirty hands.

Are yours clean?
Are yours fresh?
Are yours true?
Are you someone that I could get used to?

The blending of our spaces feels positive and free. I'll continue to allow you to reach the untouchable parts of me. Titles don't always appear in the form of words; some titles are created within our own hearts.

Miscarry

I felt you fall
out of me with
simultaneous
feelings of relief
and despair. I
wanted you but
wasn't ready
for you. We're
both better off
without each
other. I've never
been so thankful
to release what I
could no longer
carry.

Showtime

Grief feels like standing on a stage before a sold-out crowd but only noticing the empty seats. Everyone else is amazed at the sold-out crowd while you know there are still a few missing. The curtain closes, and amidst all the celebration you're left with a sinking feeling.

There will always be reminders; grieving doesn't have any rules. Life is a journey, and process is part of growing. Truth matters, and adventure awaits, all because of love. We wouldn't be where we are without some heartbreak along the way.

We'd never want to try anything again if we didn't know that the butterfly feelings can exist. If there's never an end, there's no room for beginnings. After every curtain closes, the lights will always go up again.

Emotional Olympics

Crying on the couch is like doing a bunch of reps at the gym. You don't know the depth of hard work until emotional labor begins, and just when you think you've gone as far as you can, a realization hits. You've barely broken the surface. Healing requires all the energy you've got left and rest is the only replenishment.

We all deserve gold medallions. If grieving were a profession, I'd qualify for a tenure position.

Clockwork Resignation

Time waits for no one, not
even the broken-hearted.
Forward motion even while
picking up the pieces. I've
submitted my resignation;
your healing involves my
absence.

Enneagram Status

I'm a 3w4; which typically means I'm ambitious. If you follow my direction of disintegration, you'll find that I'm presently resting in a ditch of apathy and disengagement. Some might recognize this phenomenon as me settling into my 9 tendencies.

I'm trying to figure out how I can change direction and become more integrated or cooperative just to be an even number finally. I'm aiming for a 6 mentality, but I'm still just sitting in this ditch.

Hometown Glory

I took a drive today around my old hometowns. I have a few around the Hoosier State, and so many roads lead to memories. Homes that were opened to me after escaping abuse, homes that I wasn't ready for while having no money for heat. Homes that helped me heal and trust again to lead me to my first home all on my own. In that home I learned how to be alone.

I learned how to care for my needs. I learned how to trust myself. I didn't even need to drive down that road because I still carry all of those lessons within me. Never forget the roads that brought you to where you are; they might be the same roads that will take you where you want to be.

Breaking Point

I finally let the levee break. I finally released the build-up of hot tears pushed down hour after hour, day after day. Every appearance that I was supposed to make was ignored. Every chore I created for myself was a mess left for another day. Every phone call was left unanswered. Every standard I hold for myself, I extended grace. At the end of every day, I am only human. A human that has used up all mortal energy and is ready for retreat.

This grief can only seem to be defined in pieces with no big picture to be made. There are tiny shards that impale me, and with each wound I dress, a new part is revealed. It looks similar to ones that have been felt before, but each tiny piece holds a different memory.

All these broken pieces, and somehow each meaning is known. They are shrapnels of missing that abide within me. Sometimes they are so large and sharp that they threaten my mobility, creating injuries that require an immediate response. The wound is always present, but there's no active bleed.

Recovery begins until the next broken piece is found.

Road Less Traveled

Our future is filled with uncertain pathways. Learn to give your love to the deserving. Learn to give your time to the worthy. Trust yourself and have confidence in the journey you're taking. Everyone's path is different. You may need to walk alone at times, but it won't be for long.

Handling

I'm not handling anything because I don't want to.

I'm tired of always handling this or that.

I'm okay to just sit back.

Whatever will be will be.

Whatever is to come will come.

I can't change the future any more than I can change the past.

I'm just proud that I have come this far after once standing

at

death's

door.

Mindfulness Exercise

I believe we can transport ourselves outside of our own reality if we just give ourselves enough time and space. Give it a try. After reading these words, close your eyes. Allow yourself to dream. Think about the feeling of endless possibility. What colors are surrounding you? Who is standing next to you? What does the air feel like? What are the smells that are surrounding you? Don't let yourself get distracted. Focus on your breath. Breathe.

Keep going deep inside the space of endless possibility. Do you feel a smile on your face? Have you obtained a thought that has been hiding inside your brain? Have you caught a glimpse of a dream resting inside your chest?

Feel it, hear it, connect with your breath, feel your heartbeat. That is life. You are here. You are still here, so you might as well make the most of it.

Something About Letting Go

It's rarely a feeling you want to embrace. When you're holding on so tight, the release never seems to come naturally. Moving on is an endless journey. Moment after moment of singling out grief, making it more memorable while feeling its lasting impact.

Release feels like taking flight. An anxiousness settles into the stomach as the weight of knowing the necessity of what is about to be faced. Once you level out, you can't help but experience the simultaneous feelings of missing what you've left behind while embracing what lies ahead.

You can't go forward if you're stuck looking back. Be the change you needed before the moment of impact. At some point, we have to stop making the same mistakes twice. We know these facts are part of life, so just start living through the missing and stop avoiding the lessons. Let go, while keeping on. Forward is the only place to go from here.

Bodywork

I'm learning to be okay being in this body. This body that rarely moves in the ways I need it to let alone how I want it to. This body that requires so much of my time and energy without any kind of reciprocity. There are prisoners locked away with more freedom than what this body allows me. This body causes me to stumble from time to time creating resentment from the inside. This body that requires explanation without any promise of understanding. This body that requires me to make a home out of a shell that is broken and worn down. This body that belongs to be but isn't always a friend to me. This body that I must constantly learn and unlearn intimately in hopes of finding release and forgiveness for every emotion I allowed to stay trapped inside of me.

> This body is mine.
> This body is mine.
> This body is accepted.
> This body takes time.
> This body is mine.

We're getting reacquainted, slowly but surely; learning to trust one another again. This body feels betrayed, and for that, I take full responsibility. I quit believing in its capabilities, and now it's full of resistance. It's been time to release for a long time, time to let go, time to fully process, time to remember all that's been locked away. It's hard to know what the truth is at times or what story has just been created in my mind, but we're talking again; a conversation between my body and me.

> This body is mine.
> This body is mine.
> This body is accepted.
> This body takes time.
> This body is mine.

Together, But Apart

One Day I'm Gonna Wake Up Older
Than My Mother Ever Was

It wasn't until recently that I started to believe that I didn't have to die just because she did. Being in this decade, the same one where she lost her life, doesn't always feel right. My mother's story is not mine, although we are closely woven. I'm allowing myself to unravel from believing that my life also deserves to be taken.

Perpetually Homeless

In the past five years I have lived in seven different houses. Seven different houses that have never felt like home. It's no wonder I feel more at home on the road or in the skies. I have lived in so many houses where the inhabitants don't even speak to one another. They don't know one another's language and they don't even try to learn it. I've lived in so many houses where I spend hours trying to learn the dialect of the ones I dwell with while they continue to yell obscenities that I cannot even begin to understand.

Imagine walking past someone you love without even exchanging a glance. Each house feels more like a hostel, both the feeling and the dwelling. There are pots covering the always heated stove, but never a warning as to which one is likely to blow. I've learned to find peace in being an inner peace, a gifted peace. Peace as a home and I am the house.

Rising Thoughts

When I went to sleep, she was alright. I woke up and lost my breath at the sight of her no longer living. Everything seemed to happen too fast. I never imagined an ambulance ride would be my transport to my grandmother's gravesite. There were no sirens on the way there or back; it was the most silent ride other than the rattle of the stretcher where my grandfather sat in the back.

How are the most surreal moments always attached to my life? I always seem to have the storybook experiences with no happy endings in sight.

I wish I could stop thinking about the last week of July 2021, but it's so imprinted within my memory banks. No matter how far I remove myself from that place the memories come rushing back. I want to remember them living, but I had to sit for so long with their death that I can't seem to get the stench off of me, and it's caused me to feel no sense of urgency to begin moving on to whatever is next.

Praying

And here I am praying for you.
Praying for you to see the light, praying for you to fight,
praying for you to rise. Praying for you to become honest
enough with yourself to become honest with others.
Praying for you to let love in.
Praying for peace, praying for understanding, praying for a way
to be made. Here I am praying for you so fiercely.
Praying for an open heart,
praying for healing thoughts.
And here I am praying for you; again.

Here I am praying for you; again.
Here I am praying for you to have enough.
I wish you enough music to fill the silence that scares you.
I wish you enough laughter to balance out the tears.
I wish you enough healing to protect you through life's pains.
I wish you enough strength to carry your load.
I wish you enough quiet to find peace amidst the loud.
I wish you enough love to fill the spaces of yourself that you
hate. I wish you enough peace to find understanding for
yourself. Here I am wishing for you; again.

Here I am praying for you; again.
It's not until I say amen that I see that all of these wishes and
prayers are for me to finally let love in.

Men of Sand

Women of the sea with sunshine seeping into skin, darkening the already golden glow. Water in the form of recycled tears hydrates the dry bones of sorrow. It should evaporate quickly when spreading to reach out in the desert. Men of the sand cannot care for women of the sea. Her waves will disperse his grains, and there need not be battles to the death in love.

Pour Me Out

Sometimes I wonder what it would look like if I could physically pour myself out, but I think it would depend on whether I emptied myself out from the bottom or top. The depths of me hold so many sights unseen, and I'm unsure if I'd even be able to adequately describe what is in front of me. The surface would be a displacement of all the good things. The magic in purple tones, the joy in orange hues, the thickness of my poetic spirit pouring out slowly with a honey essence like the way my words flow from my lips.

I think there would be plenty that wouldn't want to come out as if it's all stuck firmly at the bottom because some things are better left unseen. Maybe if we shook and squeezed and worked hard enough, we might be able to empty the whole of me out. We'd see pain, the color of galaxies dripping out like a slow sludge that isn't quite sure how to move because it's been inside for so long. Pieces stuck on the bottom of it all. There might even be chunks that look like lava rocks still holding some of their heat from anger that had nowhere else to go.

I don't think that it would be a pretty sight, but I'm confident it would be hard to turn your eyes away from because surely if you can see it all laid out then there would be a way to touch and heal it all. Maybe even mix it all together so that it balances itself out a little better. I've never been completely poured out, but I'm trying in hopes of fully healing and living the life I desire.

Forgiveness

I recently learned that remission is a synonym for forgiveness. Sometimes love requires recovery and sometimes forgiving requires distance. Sometimes you don't see the purpose until you're on the other side of the pain. Sometimes that pain can last a lifetime.

Until you've recovered enough to face those you love, let go of whatever is holding you back from being free. Purpose may not be revealed until your last days.

Jonah

I've been swallowed up by something larger than myself,

and that

is

where

my

faith

is

found.

A Poem That Became a Prayer

I've never been so tired while simultaneously being fully awake. Living your dreams really makes it hard to sleep, and if I am my ancestors' wildest dreams, then my descendants are already my greatest victory.

What's already been written is far beyond any of my earthly understanding, but somehow, I've been given a knowing. Every accolade my mother ever spoke over me continues to be unveiled. Knowing who you are feels different when you finally start believing.

They say there's power in a name. Korie Amanda: God's Peace Deserving to Be Loved. It also means Stephanie's Greatest Victory, her greatest accomplishment, and the core of her legacy. I am the daughter my mother always dreamed of. As I follow the steps of those who have gone before me while blazing a trail for all who will use my steps to get their footing,

I feel a sense of a calling, much greater than any duty. This high honor of any earthly being. I give thanks to the God who made me and the mother who carried me.

Here's to the journey of a never-ending story.

Battles

Battles test your endurance. Battles test your loyalties. Battles test your patience, strength and faith. Battles test you. Even battles we wage within ourselves are not defeated alone. There are armies that pray over us, warriors that fight with us, moments where our painful cries are healed and answered by the angels that protect us. In the midst of battles, there is destruction and injury, but then the rebuilding begins. A foundation becomes stronger than ever before when built up one the remains of victory.

Standing in the Gap

I keep having moments where I feel souls stand in the gap
for me. It's always the moments where I feel I can't possibly
continue, the same moments where grief feels insurmountable,
and my breath catches while I try to remember how to get
to the next inhale and exhale. Blow after blow after blow I
know, even when I can't fully stand if I just lift my head to the
heavens. Relief will find me. Gratitude to the souls standing
in the gap for me, holding the pain that I can't seem to bear
while saying the prayers of my heart that my mound cannot
yet recite.

A Love I Prayed For

A   love   that   grows   in   both   directions.

The kind of love with deep roots and radiant blooms.

A love that challenges and teaches.

A love that tests patience and earns trust.

A love with pure and honest reciprocity.

A love that leaves room while holding fast.

A love that syncs back up after skipping a beat.

A love honoring culture while creating ancestry.

A love so revolutionary that each

I love you

s   t   r   e   t   c   h   e   s

on

through

eternity.

Hope

Hope is all around, even in the most unlikely spaces and paces. It can be seen in the eyes of a child. It can be heard in the voice of a love awaiting their union. It is held in the arms of each new parent and within each beat of our hearts. Hope is all around; think of where you feel it. Think of where you see it. Do you feel it rising in your chest? Do you believe in its promise? It's waiting for you. Hope is here.

Even when everything falls apart, it's in the waiting of it all falling back together again. Hope imagined and restored. Hope is living within your heart. Think of hope in future tense. What if who you hope to be is who you already are?

I Shall Not Want

Even when seated at a table full of enemies, I shall not want. Those enemies will watch me eat, and I will be full. Even when discouragement knocks on my door, I shall not want. Encouragement always finds me, and I will be renewed. Even when the impossible is all I see, I shall not want. Endless possibility always arrives, and I am skilled in acceptance.

Even when I feel the weight of emotions, I shall not want. My body has endured many storms, and rest will find me when needed. Even when I can barely keep my head above, I shall not want. Treading water is nothing new, and the waves will always carry me. Even when my cup is on the brink of empty, I shall not want. It has never run dry, and overflow is meant for me.

REST

I don't have to earn rest.
I don't have to earn rest.
I don't have to earn rest.
I don't have to earn rest.
I don't have to earn rest.
I don't have to earn rest.
I don't have to earn rest.
I don't have to earn rest.
I don't have to earn rest.
I don't have to earn rest.
I don't have to earn rest.
I don't have to earn rest.
I don't have to earn rest.
I don't have to earn rest.
I don't have to earn rest.
I don't have to earn rest.
I don't have to earn rest.
I don't have to earn rest.
I don't have to earn rest.
I don't have to earn rest.
I don't have to earn rest.
I don't have to earn rest.
I don't have to earn rest.
I don't have to earn rest.
I don't have to earn rest.
I don't have to earn rest
I don't have to earn rest.
I don't have to earn rest.
I don't have to earn rest.
I don't have to earn rest.
I don't have to earn rest.
I don't have to earn rest.

I do not have to earn rest.

Reclamation of Joy

Joy has always belonged to you. It is yours to experience, enjoy, claim, and express to the absolute fullest extent. I hope you never catch yourself covering your smile or hiding your laugh. Your joy belongs to you.

You own every right to share your joy in the form of a laugh or a grin from ear to ear. Never forget who you are. You are who you should never forget.

Season to season, this truth will always remain, joy has always been yours to claim.

Oceanic Tendencies

I'd be perfectly content forever resting where the waves touch the shore, flowing in and out with each breeze, always shimmering in the sunshine even amidst storms. I'd keep my peace because I'm accustomed to facing what's bigger than me.

I often wonder if it's calmer in the center of it all, if there is a stillness that can be found once you're no longer standing on the shore. I'm sure there's a subtle rock of The Ocean's natural sway, but surely there's some ease to be found when your feet can no longer touch the ground; when you can give way to rest and finally allow yourself to be carried by the waves.

I see so much of myself whenever I look out to The Sea; the endless beyond, a vastness that reflects the depths of me. A force only to be feared when misunderstood or met with irreverence. It's always welcoming when trust is reciprocated.

Somehow The Ocean always quiets the fire inside of me.

Suffer Well

I am having a hard time with the reality that I am the only survivor left in my immediate family. I am only 31 years of age, and I'm not even sure what to do with myself most days. The weight of grief often becomes too much to bear, so my goal each day has been to simply live, while never wanting to live without them. I looked forward to sharing my victories and my life with all of them. Now, I must adjust to looking forward to living a life that honors them. There isn't a day that goes by where I don't feel like they should still be here, but God has always known better than I.

Most days, I can't believe that this is my life; most days I wish it wasn't. I'm just trying to make it through to whatever is next while leaving this world better than I found it. Of course my body aches, this life has been a war zone. I've taken bullet after bullet and somehow lived to tell about it. I am a living, breathing miracle intended to suffer well.

I have come to know sorrow. I invite spirituality into this suffering in hopes of giving purpose to the pain. It is not all for nothing. There are multiple chairs at this table of suffering, and I make room for everything. Joy, sorrow, anger, regret, fear, excitement, stillness, distraction; any emotion or phenomenon you can name. I invite them all into this experience with fullness and understanding that they are all necessary for my survival story. This is still only my beginning.

Acknowledgements

This book would not have been possible without the immense support from those who love me, regardless of any time and space that exists. To my family, thank you for loving me despite not always understanding me. Thank you to my REAL FRIENDS! Y'all have held me through the endless waves of grief that hit me - You are my chosen family who has kept me from drowning. You have been my breeze in the driest desert. Thank you for believing that I could bring this book to life even when I didn't always believe in myself. Thank you to Terin, my partner in business and life, your patience through this process gave me the room I needed to grieve and grow.

I am endlessly thankful to my patrons who support me month after month while keeping the vision sustained through their monthly subscriptions. To every person who contributed and supported Queen Spirit, your belief impacted me on the deepest level. Creating zines for the past four years gave me the affirmations needed to piece together this book. I owe a huge thank you to The Indiana Arts Commission for their support of artists via On-Ramp. Their grant was a great financial help in bringing this book to our hands.

I feel I should write a book of gratitude rather than some paragraphs. I am continuously in awe of the love that carries me through all that life sends my way. In every valley and on every mountain, God has remained. I am grateful. To those I began grieving this year, thank you for loving me so well that the absence of you can never be replaced. I am forever changed for the better by the time we shared.

And to you, dear reader, thank you for supporting this dream of mine. Thank you for taking the time to move through living and grieving with me through these pages in your hands. Your support keeps my dreams alive.

ABOUT THE AUTHOR

Korie Griggs is a writer who believes words are to be cherished and never wasted. She facilitates healing through the vulnerable storytelling of her life through poetry. She invites you to be part of her story while challenging you to reflect upon your own. Korie is a writer who consistently learns who she is while journeying through grief. She cherishes her deep ancestral roots and allows them to guide her through all of the brutalities and blessings that life offers. Korie is a nationally published writer and a Midwestern zine curator and publisher. As an Indiana native, she enjoys creating close to home or in the presence of wide-open nature experiences. Life has been her greatest teacher, and words have been her dearest friend. She hopes that you find safety and healing within her writing.